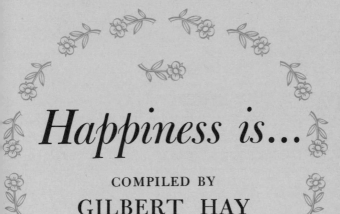

Happiness is...

COMPILED BY

GILBERT HAY

AN ESSANDESS SPECIAL EDITION

New York 1967

ACKNOWLEDGMENTS

For arrangements made with various authors and publishing houses where copyrighted material was permitted to be reprinted and for the courtesy extended by them, the following acknowledgments are gratefully made. All possible care has been taken to trace the ownership of every selection included and to make full acknowledgment for its use. If any errors have accidentally occurred, they will be corrected in subsequent editions, provided notification is sent to the publisher.

Murray Banks, for permission to use his material, copyright 1951 by Murray Banks.

The Estate of Albert Einstein, for permission to use material by Albert Einstein.

Judge Jonah J. Goldstein, President, Grand St. Boys' Association, for permission to use his material.

Harper & Row, Publishers, for permission to use material from *The Treasure Chest* and *Words of Life*, edited by Charles L. Wallis; and for material from *Live Your Life*, compiled by Walter A. Heiby.

Houghton Mifflin Company, for permission to use material by John Burroughs from *A Treasury of The Art of Living*, edited by Sidney Greenberg, copyright © 1963 by Hartmore House.

Aaron N. Meckel, for permission to use material from his book, *Living Can Be Exciting*, copyright © 1956 by E. P. Dutton & Co., Inc.

Ivan Obolensky, Inc., for permission to use material from *Five Minutes to Happiness* by Maxwell Maltz, copyright © 1962 by Ivan Obolensky, Inc.

Prentice-Hall, Inc., for permission to use material from *Distilled Wisdom* by Alfred Armand Montapert, copyright © 1964 by Alfred Armand Montapert.

Most folks are about as happy
as they make up their minds to be.

ABRAHAM LINCOLN

Happiness is
a thing to be practiced,
like the violin.

JOHN LUBBOCK

Happiness is
helping others!

Happiness must not be thought of
as a distant goal.
Unless we can learn to be happy
this very minute
we will probably never be happy.

Happiness is like a butterfly.
The more you chase it and chase it
     directly—
the more it will always just elude you.
But if you sit down quietly
and turn your attention to other things,
then it comes and softly sits on your
     shoulder!

DR. MURRAY BANKS

He enjoys much
who is thankful for little.
A grateful mind
is both a great and happy mind.

THOMAS SECKER

Success is getting what you want;
happiness is wanting what you get.

We act as though
comfort and luxury
were the chief requirements
of life,
when all we need
to make us really happy
is something
to be enthusiastic about.

CHARLES KINGSLEY

To do something, however small,
to make others happy,
is the highest ambition,
the most elevating hope,
which can inspire a human being.

JOHN LUBBOCK

We die daily—
happy those
who daily come to life as well.

GEORGE MACDONALD

Happy is the man who can enjoy the
    small things,
the common beauties, the little
    day-by-day events;
sunshine on the fields, birds on the bough,
breakfast, dinner, supper,
the daily paper on the porch,
a friend passing by.
So many people who go afield for
    enjoyment
leave it behind them at home.

DAVID GRAYSON

I don't know
what your destiny will be,
but one thing I know,
the only ones among you
who will be really happy
are those who have sought
and found how to serve.

ALBERT SCHWEITZER

Happy the man who has broken
the chains which hurt the mind,
and has given up worrying
once and for all.

OVID

The harvest of happiness
is most often reaped
by the hands of helpfulness.

GILBERT HAY, M.S.SS.T.

The secret of happiness and prosperity,
in this world
as in the world to come,
lies in thinking of
the welfare of others first,
and not taking one's self
too seriously.

JAMES H. KINDLEBERGER

You are not likely to find the flowers
of happiness around the corner
if you fail to see those now at your feet.

There is a vast difference
between happiness and pleasure.
Pleasure is a false face
that is more often the mask
of discontent than of happiness.

Everybody really knows what to do
to have his life filled with joy.
What is it?
Quit hating people; start loving them.
Quit being mad at people; start liking
     them.
Quit doing wrong;
quit being filled with fear.
Quit thinking about yourself
and go out and do something for other
     people.

*Everybody knows what you have to do
to be happy.
But the test lies in the final words:
"If you know these things,
happy are you if you do them."*

NORMAN VINCENT PEALE

One of the most tragic things I know
about human nature
is that all of us tend to put off living.
We dream of some magical rose garden
over the horizon—
instead of enjoying the roses
that are blooming
outside our window today.

DALE CARNEGIE

Every job has drudgery,
whether it is in the home,
in the professional school
or in the office.
The first secret of happiness
is the recognition of
this fundamental fact.

M. C. McINTOSH

Domestic happiness depends
upon the ability
to overlook.

ROY L. SMITH

Let the weakest,
let the humblest remember
that in his daily course he can,
if he will,
shed around him almost a heaven.
Kind words, sympathizing attentions,
watchfulness against
wounding men's sensitiveness—
these cost but little,
but are priceless in their value.
Are they not almost staples
of our daily happiness?

From hour to hour,
from moment to moment,
we are supported, blest,
by small kindnesses.

FREDERICK W. ROBERTSON

We begin to walk
on the road to happiness
when we learn the art
of relaxation.
When we learn
that relaxation is a habit
we can all acquire,
a healthy habit every day,
like brushing our teeth.

MAXWELL MALTZ

In the pursuit of happiness
half the world is on the wrong scent.
They think it consists
in having and getting,
and in being served by others.
Happiness is really found in giving
and in serving others.

HENRY DRUMMOND

One of the hardest lessons
we have to learn in this life,
and one that many persons never learn,
is to see the divine,
the celestial, the pure
in the common—the near at hand.
To see that heaven lies about us
here in this world.

JOHN BURROUGHS

He who can no longer
pause to wonder
and stand rapt in awe
is as good as dead.

ALBERT EINSTEIN

The world is full
of wonders and miracles
but man takes his little hand
and covers his eyes
and sees nothing.

ISRAEL BAAL SHEM

Before we set our hearts
  too much upon anything,
Let us examine how happy
  are they who already possess it.

LA ROCHEFOUCAULD

The measure of our happiness
is the gifts of ourselves
which we give to others.

Happiness is a perfume
you cannot pour on others
without getting a few drops
on yourself.

RALPH WALDO EMERSON

Enjoy as many of your daily tasks
as you can.
Do the others and enjoy
having them behind you.

Happiness, I have discovered, is nearly
always a rebound from hard work.
It is one of the follies of men
to imagine that they can enjoy
mere thought, or emotion, or sentiment.
As well try to eat beauty!
For happiness must be tricked!
She loves to see men at work.
She loves sweat, weariness, self-sacrifice.
She will be found not in palaces
but lurking in cornfields and factories
and hovering over littered desks;
she crowns the unconscious head
of the busy child.

If you look up suddenly from hard work
you will see her,
but if you look too long
she fades sorrowfully away.

DAVID GRAYSON

I say, "It's a darn good day
when a man can put on his shoes
and go to work."

JOHN BURNES

Let's talk about our happiness.
By telling others how happy we are,
we will discover that we are very happy.
We'll also help our listeners
to think happy thoughts.
The happiness we induce in others induces,
in turn, greater happiness in ourselves.

Happiness exists where there is,
in addition to the things
that bring satisfaction and contentment,
a conscious awareness
that one has these things.
Most of us have the first qualification
for happiness—we have
an abundance of blessings.
It is in the second area
that we fall short: we fail to recognize
the fact that we have all these things.
Through such recognition we achieve
happiness.

Not what we have,
but what we enjoy
constitutes our abundance.

J. PETIT-SENN

The man who has found something
he can be enthusiastic about
has found a fountainhead of happiness.

He who is really kind
will never be unhappy.

All of us have the capacity
to manufacture trouble anywhere,
any time, out of anything or out of nothing.
Happy persons decline to use this ability.

The happiest life,
seen in perspective,
can hardly be better than
a stringing together of odd
little moments.

NORMAN DOUGLAS

Here is a universal characteristic
of happy, successful people
I can easily assume.
I will tell others what is right about people;
I will keep to myself what I think is wrong.

If we would change our lives
we must first change our attitudes.
Happiness is not created by what happens
to us but by our attitude toward each
    happening.

Welcome your problems.
Through solving problems we gain
life's greatest satisfactions.

We pose an unrewarding question
if we ask ourselves, "What am I getting
out of my religion—my marriage—
     my job?"
Instead of thinking, "What can I get?"
why not think, "What can I give?"
It is the attitude of giving
that leads to a full life.

Every man, woman, and child on this earth
has an overwhelming desire to be loved,
to be wanted, to be appreciated.
To the extent that we can fulfill
this desire will we give happiness
and find happiness ourselves.

Unless we find beauty and happiness
in our backyard
we will never find them
in the mountains.

Happiness isn't found
in searching for it.
It comes quietly
while we are helping others.

A man's contentment lies
in enthusiastic appreciation
for the things he has.
A man's misery lies
in excessive desire
for the things he has not.

Take what God gives, O heart of mine,
  And build your house of happiness.
Perchance some have been given more;
  But many have been given less.
The treasure lying at your feet,
  Whose value you but faintly guess,
Another builder, looking on,
  Would barter heaven to possess.

B. Y. WILLIAMS

Happiness is
the one thing in life
that multiplies by division.
The more happiness one
gives to others
the more he has himself.

JUDGE JONAH J. GOLDSTEIN

Here's an answer to boredom
and unhappiness:
find a way to help someone.

The sunset does not give us
the gift of beauty.
We bring the beauty to the sunset.
In bringing the gift
of a happy smile to others,
we help give ourselves happiness.

Happiness is like a crystal,
  Fair and exquisite and clear,
Broken in a million pieces,
  Shattered, scattered far and near.

  Now and then along life's pathway,
    Lo! some shining fragments fall;
  But there are so many pieces,
    No one ever finds them all.

PRISCILLA LEONARD

Be happy with what you have and are,
be generous with both,
and you won't have to hunt for happiness.

WILLIAM E. GLADSTONE

Happy is he who by love's sweet song
Is cheered today as he goes along.
Happier is he who believes that tomorrow
Will ease all pain and take away all sorrow.
Happiest he who on earthly sod
Has faith in himself, his friends, and God.

The happiness of life is made up
of minute fractions—the little,
soon forgotten charities of a kiss
or a smile, a kind look,
a heartfelt compliment,
and the countless infinitesimals
of pleasurable and genial feeling.

SAMUEL T. COLERIDGE

Contentment, and indeed usefulness,
comes as the infallible result
of great acceptances, great humilities—
of not trying to make ourselves
this or that, but of surrendering ourselves
to the fullness of life—
of letting life flow through us.
To be used—that is
the sublimest thing we know.

DAVID GRAYSON

No one is happy unless
he is reasonably well satisfied with himself,
so that the quest for tranquillity
must of necessity
begin with self-examination

WILLIAM S. OGDON

As I look around me, I seem to find
that the one thing which deepens life,
which gives it resonance,
which brings it great joy,
is the putting of one's self
outside one's self
into another self or personality.

HARRY A. OVERSTREET

If you are alive and happy today,
that is enough.
Tomorrow never comes until it is today.
There's no reason
why each succeeding day
should not be as happy,
or happier,
than your yesterdays
if you mentally picture
a continuation of this happiness
in your future.

HAROLD SHERMAN

Happy homes
are built
of blocks
of patience.

HAROLD E. KOHN

Every day stop before something
beautiful long enough to say,
"Isn't that b-e-a-u-t-i-f-u-l!"

ALICE FREEMAN PALMER

Very little is needed
to make a happy life.
It is all within yourself,
in your way of thinking.

MARCUS AURELIUS

Not what we have or are or do,
but our attitude toward
what we have and are and do,
is what makes us happy or unhappy.

Your living is determined
not so much by what life brings to you
as by the attitude you bring to life;
not so much by what happens to you
as by the way your mind looks at what
   happens.
Circumstances and situations do color life,
but you have been given the mind
to choose what the color shall be.

JOHN HOMER MILLER

Keep gratitude alive in your heart.
Try living on "Thanksgiving Street."
Reckon up your mercies and you will feel
an inner kindling of soul.
People will be glad at the sight of you.
And who knows?
Perhaps even the heart of the
infinite Giver of every good
and perfect gift will rejoice.

AARON N. MECKEL

Happiness is the full use of your powers
along lines of excellence
in a life affording scope.

JOHN F. KENNEDY

Having more material things
does not produce happiness.
Happiness comes through striving
to get the most out of
what we already have.

You will find, as you look back
upon your life, that the moments
that stand out are the moments when
you have done things for others.

HENRY DRUMMOND

A source of unhappiness, or failure
to achieve full happiness,
is the habit of invidious comparison.
To one who constantly compares,
there was once a pie more
delicious than this one,
a day that was sunnier,
a profit that was greater,
a girl who was prettier,
a climate elsewhere
that seemed more favorable.
The act of comparison
should be restricted to the arts,
to scientific analyses,

to other fields employing quantitative
relationships and to phenomena where
people are not involved.
Comparison that involves people
and their acts
and those circumstances intimately
connected with our happiness
must be purged from our thinking.
Happiness is achieved through enjoyment
of the present situation
undiluted by thoughts of similar
circumstances that appear more favorable
when viewed in retrospect.

We must not look outside
for happiness,
but in ourselves, in our own minds.
"The kingdom of God
is within you."

JOHN LUBBOCK

Above all things,
reverence yourself.

PYTHAGORAS

Happiness grows
at our own firesides,
and is not to be picked
in stranger's gardens.

DOUGLAS JERROLD